OVERCOMER

BY

EVANGELIST THERESA LAWRENCE

LIFE TO LEGACY, LLC

Overcomer
By: Theresa Lawrence Copyright 2022

ISBN: 978-1-947288-72-0

All rights reserved solely by the author. Except where designated, the author certifies that all contents are original and do not infringe upon the legal rights of any other person. No part of this book may be reproduced in any form without permission in writing from the publisher, except in the case of brief quotations embodied in critical articles or reviews.

All Scriptures are taken from the King James Version.

Cover and interior photography by: Will Lewis IV.

Printed in the United States of America

10 9 8 7 6 5 4 3 2 1

Cover design by: Legacy Designs, Inc.

Published by: Life To Legacy, LLC
P.O. Box 1239
Matteson, IL 60443

www.Life2Legacy.com

TABLE OF CONTENTS

Dedication		4
Introduction		6
1	Letting Go of Your Past	9
2	Teenage Mom	15
3	Forgiving	21
4	Rejection	27
5	Dealing with Death	31
6	Endurance	37
7	Love	43
About the Author		49

Dedication

I would like to honor a few people along the way who have helped me in my journey with Christ.

Thank you to my former Pastor Bishop Horace E. Smith, M.D. of Apostolic Faith Church for teaching me sound doctrine and the importance of loving God's Word, and the necessity of prayer and spending quality time with God. I Love you.

I would like to thank one of my oldest sisters, for leading me to Christ. Love you.

I would like to thank Evangelist Barbara Ellzey for always encouraging me to operate in my gifts by asking me to join our prayer line to pray for others. You also help me with becoming an altar worker at Apostolic Faith Church. I Love you and will never forget how God used you in life.

A big thank you to sister Kimberly Clifton for always supporting the gift and calling on my life. Thank you for your prayers over the years. I love you.

Thank you to every family member, friend, co-worker from across the world who have supported the calling on my life. I love you all.

Thank you to my photographer Will Lewis IV.

Introduction

What does it mean to be an overcomer? According to *Dictionary.com*, the word *overcomer* means to *prevail, gain victory, to conquer and defeat.* In John 5:4-5, Jesus describes overcoming when he states, "For whatever is born of God overcomes the world; and this is the victory that has overcome the world—our faith. Who is the one who overcomes the world, but he who believes that Jesus is the Son of God?"

Throughout the Scriptures, there are many testimonies of those who have overcome great odds and obstacles such as; Daniel, Joseph, Moses, Joshua, Ruth, Naomi and many more. Back in Bible times, these men and women of valor struggled with the same trials of everyday life just as we do today. They faced the death of loved ones, rejection, betrayal, and envy. They experienced the trauma of abandonment and loss when circumstances arose that caused them to be raised by those other than their own family. However, despite the depth of trials and tribulations they experienced, these overcomers give us hope to keep our trust in the Lord. Every last one of them was delivered from the clutches of despair that sought to bind them. This is why the Lord encourages us to "...be of good courage, I have overcome the world."

In Revelation 11:12, the Bible states, "...And they overcame him by the blood of the Lamb, and by the word of their testimony...." Therefore, in this book, I will share my testimony of how God gave me the strength to overcome even though after the age of nine, I was not raised by my biological parents. This is my testimony of how God brought me through the valley of the shadow of death, during the death of my father and brother, who both died from cancer. This is my story, of all the hurt and rejection I endured being a teenaged mom, but through it all, God taught me how to forgive.

No matter how prepared you think you are, life can catch you by surprise. However, if you walk by faith and not by sight, the Lord is faithful to empower you to overcome any giant that attempts to block your success. The Bible declares, "greater is He that is in you than he that is in the world." I pray that this book will be a blessing and a source of encouragement to all who read it, so that you too, will be a powerful "Overcomer."

1
Letting Go of the Past

I come from a large family. My mother and father had a total of nine children, and I was blessed to be the seventh child. Though my childhood days are long past, I still have the title as "the baby sister." I was always a child who loved to talk and speak my mind, it all makes since now because I love ministering to others. Growing up wasn't easy for me. There were many difficult times but my mom and dad did the best they could with raising so many kids at one time. Even though a few of my older siblings had already left home, we still had large family struggles.

There were some obvious signs that our family had financial difficulties. We didn't have the latest clothing or gym shoes. Often times, the clothes we wore became the reason we were ridiculed and even bullied. Kids teased us because we were wearing pro-wings and light up shoes from Payless. At other times, me and my sisters would get bullied walking home from school for no apparent reason. When my dad wasn't busy or working, he would walk to the school to escort us back home. We walked because we never owned a vehicle. Our living arrangements were not the best either, we lived in the projects and apartments as well.

However, when I was about 9 years old things took a turn for the worst. Due to my mother's addiction, we were removed from my mother's care and we moved from house to house. Then I moved in with a relative, but things didn't work out. After that didn't work out, we were placed in the system. Then we moved to a group home where we stayed for about a year until someone would take custody of us, and move us to a foster home.

While all the other kids who were not in the system, were enjoying a normal life with their parents, at the time, we were only allowed to have visitation with ours. That was truly heartbreaking and traumatizing. Looking back at everything, I know my mom couldn't help herself after losing control over her life because of her addiction. However, even in the midst of her struggles, she still cared for us and always made sure we ate and had clean clothes. But, even though my dad worked and never had any addition issues, he had a difficult time regaining custody of us.

A year later we moved in with my aunt. I thank God for that we did not end up in a foster home. During that time, I was able to see my mom and she had just given birth to my baby brother. My dad had moved to another state where God blessed him to have a house and a good job as a store manager. We would go to visit him often and he'll come visit us in Chicago. He was a wonderful father. He was fighting to win back custody for us. Eventually, my mother got the victory over her addiction and reunited with my father. With the Lord's help, things were really looking up. However, by the time I had turned 14 is when my father was stricken with cancer. The doctors only gave him a few months to live. Sadly, he died a few months later a day before his birthday. The last time we visited him we were shocked because he had loss so much weight. I didn't know much about cancer back in 2002, but seeing my father in that condition, was the worst thing I had ever experienced in my life.

As a teenager, I didn't know how to deal with the pain, so I suppressed it and pretended that it didn't bother me. However, as I got older it began to have an impact on my life. With not having my mother around and father passing away, I felt lost. I didn't really know what it was like to truly be loved. Looking back at it, I knew it was God who carry me through all the obstacles I had encountered at such a young age. I thank God for my parents, because I wouldn't be here. I am also grateful for my aunt for taking us in, or we would have ended up in a foster home.

The Bible says that the Devil is the accuser of the brethren. If you're familiar with the book of Job, you'll see that the Devil appeared with the angels before God. That's how the enemy works. He goes to God, and he uses whatever He can to bring accusation against us. As the Bible tells us, Job was such an upright man. However, the Devil accused him of only serving God because of all the blessings God had given him. God then allowed the Devil to afflict Job but he wouldn't allow the Devil to kill him. Though I cannot compare myself to his righteousness, many of us are like Job. And just like Job, the Devil brings accusation against us, especially concerning our past.

He often reminds us of what has happened to us and about all the wrong we have done. Thank God for Jesus, because in Jesus we no longer have to feel guilty about our past. We can overcome by forgiving what has happened to us and the things we have done because when you have accepted Jesus as your Lord and Savior you are no longer bound but free. For a long time, I didn't think highly of myself. I didn't know how worthy I was until I start seeing myself the way God sees me and not the little girl of my past. I'm not my past. My past only allowed me to become better and for Christ to use me as a testimony. I challenge you to let go of your past. Know that God is for you and not against you. Whatever has happened to you in your past, can't compare to what God wants to do now and in your future.

For those of you who have been in foster care, not being raised by your own parents, God still has a plan for your life. According to Jeremiah 29:11, God declares, "I know the thoughts I think towards you says the Lord, thoughts of peace and not of evil to give you a hope and future." God loves you so much and has a plan for your life just as he had a plan for me. Regardless of what you face in life, if you allow God to mold you and fix your past. It's important to forgive your parents for the mistakes they have made. Even in the severe cases where it caused you to go into the system, regardless of what happened, you can still be victorious. God knew what He was doing from the very beginning, because He used your parents to bring you into this world.

Your life may not make much sense while you're living it out, but I promise you it's a brighter day that God wants to fulfill in your life. In Psalm 27:10, God said "…if your mother or father forsake you, that the Lord will take care of you." You're not only an overcomer just from dealing with not being raised by your parents but you're also a testimony. Walk in the calling God has place inside of you to do. You will prosper and look back and see the goodness of God giving you strength to accomplish His will in your life. Believe that God wants only the best for you, stay positive and don't let life make you *bitter* but *better*. You are an overcomer.

2
Teenage Mom

Shortly after the passing of my father, at the age of 17, I became pregnant. Being a teenaged mother, I was too embarrassed to tell others. As you could imagine, I had many people to judge me. Some ridiculed me and said I was only trying to be like my 19-year-old sister who was pregnant a couple months before me. I had major goals in life. I wanted to go to college and become a lawyer or nurse. Oftentimes when you don't have your parents around as positive role models, it's easy to look for love in all the wrong places. However, after having my daughter is when I experienced true love. She was so calm. To this day with her being 19, she's such a sweet humble young lady who loves worship music and going to church. I've tried my best to raise her in the Lord since I've been saved, she also got saved when she was 10 years old. I know God blessed me with this type of love because she's so affectionate, sweet, and loving, and definitely heaven sent.

Being a mom at an early age made me strive to do better and stay in school to get my diploma and go to college. I graduated on time and had the best grades during my senior year. Looking back at it, I was distracted by so many things. I focused on dating, going out to the clubs and just partying. I moved into my own apartment at age 18 and have been on my own ever since.

The clubs were my favorite place to go, getting drunk and men. Sometimes I wonder what my life would have been like if I didn't have my daughter. But, at the same time, I cannot imagine life without her. I went to college and took up a trade which led me to the career I am in today. I also went back to school, and now I'm close to receiving my degree in nursing.

My daughter has motivated me to want to be better in life. I've accomplished so much with her by doing things I didn't get to do as a child. She's been to Disney World, The Mall of America, New Orleans, Hollywood, Universal Studios, LA, and more places. She's had a birthday party every year which I never got to experience as a child. I don't recall many birthdays being celebrated. I've made sure to make her life much better than mine. Thanks be to God that I have done well and she has an amazing father.

She graduated from high school and now she's a freshman in college studying to be in the medical field. She has inspired me to go after all my dreams in life. God has truly favored her. My one desire from the Lord was her not to become a teen mom like I did. God has honored my request and has kept her focused in life. Although she is into boys, that has not been a distraction or issue. I have to thank God for changing my life and being able to pray for my daughter and release God's blessings and the Word over her life. It's been great growing with her. I know God is keeping her and I can be at peace knowing I've done my job as a mother to raise her in the Lord. She's not perfect, but she's nothing like I was at her age. To God be the glory for what He has done. I love you Daughter, my future Nurse.

I am writing this book to encourage teenage girls. If you are feeling like you need to find love from some young man, I encourage you to get to know who's you are first. Keep your priorities straight. At that age you should be focus on school. If you are involved in church, let God teach you how to love yourself. Allow yourself to know God and the love and plans He has for your life. Since I didn't have a Godly upbringing, at a young age, I became focused on boys. I fooled myself into believing that they really liked me, but in reality, all most of them ever wanted was sex. You must know that you're precious and valuable. If you seek the wrong type of attention, you can end up giving yourself to anyone. Go to school, focus on your career, and true love will find you when you are ready, when the time is right. Whatever you do, don't get so distracted like I was with wanting a young man to love me. The truth is God's love for you is sufficient because its true love, so deep and so strong. Even if you feel you have no one else, He's right there cheering you along to accomplish your dreams that He has placed inside of you. It's okay to enjoy your teenage years but don't get so distracted by boys.

For all of the teenagers reading this book you should know that there are so many things God wants to do in you. I know that society is teaching you who you should be. But do you know that God in heaven has thoughts and plans for you, even as a teen? My daughter is the complete opposite of me. When I was a teenager, I was involved in everything, including being on the cheer leading team in high school. I was also nominated as the best dressed among a class of 800 plus graduates. But being popular can sometimes you get you in a lot of trouble. I attracted a lot of negativity and got into several arguments and fights. I guess with being from the projects, fighting was a way of life. So, I definitely wasn't a punk! But as I look back at it I can see that what the Devil meant for evil, God meant for my good. God now uses my personality to save souls because I'm a soldier in the army of the Lord.

I love giving my testimony and talking to people about Christ. Now my daughter has been raised in church and comes from a great foundation with me and her father being in her life. I pray for her often, including her friends. God gave my daughter one true best friend, and she wasn't as popular in school because she likes to be in the background. She's very quiet. Look how God allowed her to be the opposite of me. I have seen how God has truly blessed my daughter. She has such a joyful spirit, she is not your average teenager but she's who God called her to be.

Don't be afraid to be different. Do not give in to the temptation to be like the crowd because God has called you to be unique. You don't have to follow the crowd, be who God made you to be and don't you dare think something is wrong with you because you don't fit in with others. If I can give you the greatest advice of what I've learned from being a teen mom, is not to be in a rush for love. Enjoy your younger years. I promise you, God has a plan for you. Stay hopeful and don't you ever think God doesn't want anything to do with you, because He longs to direct your life. Yes, even in your youthful years, God wants to hear from you. Looking back, I wished I knew God when I was a teen, but I thank God He didn't take His eyes off of me. Even in my mistakes, He had such a great future in store for me.

I'm so glad God's grace doesn't run out and that His mercy endures forever. Being a teen mom you feel ashamed. You feel like the world is judging you. You even feel like you failed in life because most teens are preparing for college, but I had to prepare to raise a child. Although I felt like my life was being redirected because I was a teen mom, God was actually was directing my path the whole time. To God be the glory!

3
Forgiving

If you're going to be a overcomer you must learn to forgive others who have wronged you, hurt you or caused you pain. Life is filled with so much heart ache, pain and even betrayal. Doesn't it seem like the same things Jesus endured; we also endure to this day? Jesus said if we want to be forgiven for our sins, we must forgive those who have trespassed against us.

To everyone who has ever hurt me, I forgive you. I'm not perfect and I'm sure I have hurt people in the past with my actions or words, and I have already repented. We must not hold people's past against them because these same people who hurt you, may have already asked God to forgive them. That's why we must forgive because you do not want God to hold your past against you. I'm not saying this to you so you can go back to being their best buddy. That depends on the situation. Although I'm not married yet, I'm sure marriage requires a lot of compromise and forgiveness.

I've been hurt in relationships and at times have dealt with verbal abuse. But still I had to forgive. When you forgive you actually release yourself from the hurt. When you fail to forgive anger builds up and you become bitter and develop a critical spirit. Jesus said "I have come so that you may have life, and life more abundantly." We can only experience that abundant life when we are obedient to God's Word. God knows what people have done to you, how they have hurt and misused you. In fact, He said pray for them, not get even with them. We must allow God to fight our battles.

Life is filled with disappointment from people that we did not anticipate. But do you think that God is surprised? Certainly not! However, one thing God does, is make those things work out for our good. He uses those hurtful things to make us stronger, better and more mature. He said to count it all joy when you fall into various trials, knowing that the testing of your faith produces patience. Have you ever seen a person who has a lot of patience? Well, it took a lot to get them to that point. Those who have great patience, went through some tough times to get to a point where they didn't allow every situation to make them angry.

Even when Jesus was being crucified, He said, "Father, forgive them; for they know not what they do" (Luke 23:34). Jesus understood that if only these people knew who He was, they would not have abused Him. However, even in midst of being beaten and then nailed to the Cross. He still asked the Father to forgive them. Jesus understood His assignment and the power of forgiveness.

I had an ex-boyfriend who almost got me fired from my job because of issues that transpired between us. Even though I almost lost my job, I still had to forgive him. How do I know I had truly forgiven Him? I helped him when he was in need of food. I could have turned my back on him, but it was at that moment I chose to forgive and respond in love and help him. It was at that point that I knew I had become a mature Christian. To this day, we are actually at peace with each other and still friends. It is my desire to see him in heaven one day.

"Vengeance is mine said the Lord I will repay" (Romans 12:19). Your job is to forgive. Let God deal with the rest. I just want to encourage you by saying, that forgiveness looks good on you. To every person who has ever hurt you, forgive them. Not only because God forgives you, but because you deserve your peace. As you continue to journey in life, you will be faced with challenges that require you to forgive. But never stop forgiving. Why, because the Bible says that "love covers a multitude of sins" (1 Peter 3:18). Remember what the Lord said? "Blessed are the merciful: for they shall obtain mercy (Matt. 5:7).

"To every person who has ever rejected me, overlooked me, and talked bad about me, I forgive you!"

One of my favorite stories in the Bible with forgiveness is the story of Joseph found in Genesis chapters 37-50. Joseph was favored by his father Jacob, because he was the son of his old age and the first to be born from His wife Rachel whom he loved very much. Joseph was a dreamer. God often gave him dreams about his future. But Joseph made the mistake of telling his half-brothers his dreams which caused them to become jealous. One day they sold Joseph into slavery and lied to their parents saying that he was killed by a wild animal.

Can you imagine how Joseph felt? I'm sure he was hurt, and sadden that his brothers would do something like that to him. This story may sound familiar to you but in a different way. Have you ever had to forgive someone close to you? A family member, a close friend or even a coworker? Well God favored Joseph and the Bible even said that "God was with Him." You may wonder how can God be with someone as they're going through so much in life? That's because God's plans are much bigger than our "temporary" situation.

Well because God had given Joseph the interpretation of dreams, he was able to interpret Pharaoh's disturbing dream. Pharaoh was so pleased at Joseph's ability, the he promoted him to rule Egypt while they went through a 7-year famine. Yes, through it all, God gave Joseph the favor and wisdom on how to prosper Egypt even while they experienced a famine. Well guess who ended up needing Joseph's help? His very own brothers who sold him into slavery years earlier, had to come to the his land to get food. When they came to Egypt to ask for food they had to deal with the very brother they forsook and sold into slavery. When his brothers came before Joseph, they didn't recognize Joseph, but he recognized them. However, Joseph showed mercy to them, and gave them food. He had to forgive them because He knew the Lord had been so good to him even through slavery and prison.

Joseph spent over ten years away from his family, but God knew his family would need him during those distressful times of famine. Yet, God still saw fit for Joseph to bless his brothers even though they betrayed him. Joseph was reunited with his father and God used Joseph to be a blessing to his family, and thereby saving the nation of Israel.

Wow, what a story right? Well, that's the type of forgiveness God wants us to have toward each other, because He is a God of forgiveness, and has forgiven us. If someone has hurt you to the point you feel like they are unworthy of your forgiveness, just think about how God has forgiven you. The bottom line, none of us are worthy of His forgiveness. But because of Jesus blood that was shed on the Cross, that's what God sees when we ask for forgiveness. God has given us "the ministry of reconciliation" toward one another. You can forgive that very person that caused you so much pain. Through a divine act of love, that same pain Jesus endured for us on the Cross. Because of His great act of love, He knew we would no longer be condemned but be forgiven and have eternal life. I challenge you to go deep into your heart and forgive the person who caused you so much pain. You can do it, because Christ did it for us.

Have you ever gone through a breakup and the pain wasn't going away? Well, eventually it did, and God allowed you to keep pressing on. As you press forward, press toward forgiveness in order to activate peace and freedom in your heart.

4
Rejection

Rejection can come in many different forms. You can get rejected from a relationship, a job, family, even in a church. Let's talk about rejection. I didn't really know what rejection was until I got saved. I started to look back over my life and realized "wow" I've really been rejected by a lot of different people in my life. I want to encourage you and to let you know it's normal to experience rejection However, it is important not to adopt a victim's mentality.

The Bible tells us that Jesus was rejected by his very own (John 1:11). When Jesus returned to his home town He was rejected (Luke 4:24). Luke 17:25, also tells us that Jesus had to "suffer many things and be rejected by that generation." Jesus had a purpose to fulfill in life. Although He was flesh as we are, He knew His Godly purpose. It was part of the Divine plan for Jesus to suffer many things like, being persecuted, rejected, lied on, beaten, betrayed. All this is what prepared Him for the Cross. No one took His life, but He laid down to take away the sin of the world.

When I was young, I did receive a lot of love from my siblings. I know what it's like to be rejected by a man, especially when he was unfaithful. I know what it is like to be a young person in the church serving in ministry but being overlooked because of my age. My Pastor approved of me, however, others did not. Many people judged me on my outer appearance because of the way I dressed. I was always appropriate for church, but still loved my fashion and heels. I can't help the gift God gave me. Although many accepted it, many still judged me for it. They felt that I was seeking attention and not worthy enough to operate in my gift.

I remember crying about it, but God told me to endure it and He used me to pray for many people at the altar. Some of the same people started requesting that I pray for them. If I would have let rejection take control of me, I would have never walked in my purpose in ministry. I have been ministering for a long time but now I'm a licensed minister. This is why you cannot let rejection defeat you. If you allow it, it will make you bitter causing you to develop a critical unforgiving spirit which is not like God. God wants you to walk in love, regardless of how much rejection you're experiencing. If God dwells in you, you must love, because God is love.

Yes, you will experience rejection walking with Christ. But, walking in love will allow you to overcome the enemy's plans to make you think like no one cares for you. However, the truth is there are people who really do care for you. Pray for the people who reject you because "they know not what they do." If you've been rejected by your family, love them anyway. If you're being rejected after a job interview, don't give up, your "yes" is coming. If you're being rejected by a relationship, thank God. See this as Divine protection, because God has the right one for you. If you're being rejected for Christ's sake, "count it all joy" knowing that you are a partaker in Christ's suffering. Rejection led Jesus to the Cross to fulfill His assignment. Therefore, be of good courage and fulfill your assignment too. Stay focused, Forgive and walk in love so it doesn't hinder your walk on the way to fulfilling your calling.

God is love. He never rejects you. He loves it when we talk to Him, and fellowship with Him. You are created in the image of God; you are so loved by Him. Remember how people treat you us a reflection of them, not a reflection of God. Never allow rejection cause you to not love, because when you love people you are also loving God.

You overcome rejection by accepting Christ's love for you. He died so that you may live again. John 15:13 declares, "Greater love hath no man than this, that a man lay down his life for his friends." You have a friend in Jesus. Remember, if God be for you, it doesn't matter who's against you. Receive and accept God love and He will put genuine people in your life who will truly love you. Even when loved ones reject you, God will place others that do love you in your life. The Bible declares, "…and there is a friend *that sticketh closer than a brother* (Proverbs 18:24, KJV).

Here's a few positive things that you should know about rejection. *Rejection* is often protection. *Rejection* may come in many forms in life, but I'm so glad God doesn't reject us. *Rejection* is helping you to depend on God's love. Rejection is hard but if redirects us. *Rejection* can't defeat a person who knows God is for them. *Rejection* can't stop God's plans. *Rejection* actually causes you not to settle for less than God's best for you.

5

Dealing with Death

Before I gave my life to Christ, I really didn't have any clue about death. I had heard of heaven but I didn't know what it took to get there until I got saved. Even though we are all going to die, death is a topic that most of us do not want to discuss. As I said in previous chapters, my dad died when I was 15 years old, while he was in the process of regaining custody of us.

After I got saved, I remember asking God why He allowed my father to die? All I could hear is, "you are a testimony in my ear." I didn't realize the effect my father had on me until later on in life. He was a good father. I don't have any memories of him mistreating us. So, after I got saved I learned about the saving power in John 3:16, "that God so loved the world, that He gave His only begotten Son, that whosoever believes in Him, will not perish but have everlasting life." My mother shared with me that my dad accepted Jesus as his Savior before he passed away. It was John 3:16 that she shared with him. After I heard that, till this very day, I had a great sense of peace about my father's passing. There is a sad finality about death in the physical world because we won't ever experience their physical presence any longer. It just as stated in the Bible, tells us, from dust we came, to dust we shall return (Eccl. 3:20).

We are spirit. When we leave this earth, our physical body perishes but our spirit lives forever. Now the fact that God gave us this free gift of salvation and everlasting life by accepting Jesus as our Savior, gives us an abiding peace, that when I leave this earth I'll be with my Lord. Therefore, we must repent daily, knowing Jesus requires changed behavior also. There are things we must not do in order to be able to enter the kingdom of heaven. It is vitally important that we stay right with God and repent daily of our sins.

A few years ago, my oldest brother was diagnosed with a cancer that is rare for younger people, but most people don't get until they reach their sixties. My brother was only forty. From the beginning I was making sure he went to the doctor. He had this huge lump sticking out of his chest. Like a lot of people, my brother was afraid of going to the doctor. But going to the doctor can help to detect and prevent illnesses that can get a lot worse. He was going to chemotherapy, but at some point, he stopped going. As a result, his condition got worse. He went into the hospital a few days before Christmas. We went to see him on Christmas Day. I remember his eyes were bloodshot and very red. The following day, on the 26th, he went into cardiac arrest. He stayed on life support for a few days. They kept asking my mom to pull the plug saying he's not going to make it.

I remember getting ready to walk out the room crying, suddenly one of his eyes opened. I told my mom he's not ready to go yet. So, days went by and no progress. We transferred him to Rush Hospital. He went into cardiac arrest again. At that point, his lungs, kidneys and other organs begin to shut down. The doctors kept saying he's not going to make it. They said he was one of the sickest patients in Chicago. But despite their grim prognosis, we kept praying, and believing. I kept fasting, I lost so much weight.

God often speaks to me through dreams. I had a dream that my brother woke up and was in a wheelchair. I also saw us at a funeral, but I kept going to the hospital. I remember paying attention to his monitor. I noticed that it indicated that he was only breathing at 60% percent instead of 90% where he normally was. I asked the nurse is he starting to breathe on his own? She said "yes." I came back the next day, and his eyes were wide open. I couldn't help but give God the glory.

He knew who I was, and he was in his right mind as if nothing had ever happened after being on life support for a month. He couldn't eat and had to learn how to walk again. He was in a wheelchair just as I had dreamed. He had a long way to go. He ended up going to therapy. However, he went into cardiac arrest again. His body wasn't ready. So, he was discharged and came home. On one occasion I was taking him to his doctor's appointment. However, by the time we got there his oxygen level was so low he could have died—but God. After that incident he had to carry a small oxygen machine with him but it wasn't strong enough.

When my brother was admitted to Mount Sinai Hospital, I often talked to him about God and repenting. I had given him a book to read about not fearing death. It was at that time he told me he wasn't afraid of death. At that moment in time my brother accepted Jesus as his Lord and Savior. We would have small talks about forgiving people and talked about God.

Well, he lived 3 months after he woke up. God answered my prayer, I prayed for him to walk and he did. I remember feeding him and bringing him his favorite juice. God used me in a mighty way in the last months of my brother's life. I remember the day he died. He was in hospice care at my mother's house. I wasn't going to go over that day but I went to go see him anyway. While I was there, he woke up. He was sweating profusely so I sat him up and gave him some water. I left that Saturday, by Sunday morning, my mom went to check on him, he had made his transition. I felt like he was waiting for me to visit. He looked like he was just at peace and ready to go. He was at peace. That's why I'm at peace knowing God saved him before he left us.

Although it was hard losing my oldest brother, he had endured so much in life but now he was finally at peace. God performed a miracle in his life. Even the doctors were amazed when he regained consciousness. Just as my dream revealed, I was there to help plan his funeral. It was so hard loosing him but I had comfort at the same time knowing his spirit will live forever with the Lord.

From now on, I pray that you look at death differently. Although it's so hard to lose a love one, I pray you find comfort in our Lord, knowing with him is everlasting life.

In Loving Memory

of my

Father Gerald Hill

Oldest Brother

Gregory Lawrence

Rest well to every person we have lost in the Lawrence family.

6
Endurance

In life we are faced with challenges we never see coming. The question is, how do you handle unexpected trouble? Jesus told us we will have trouble, but he's declared that He has overcome the world. God is fighting every battle for you and He's preparing you for greater things. You're not being punished but being molded and shaped for God's greater plan for your life. Endure what you're facing because the glory is at the finish line. A runner may feel pain in their legs and body, but they keep running for the prize at the finish line. Something great is about to happen to you after you endured the test. God honors faith.

So how can a woman like me still have joy, peace, strength, happiness and success after all I've been through? The answer is God and endurance.

What I have learned throughout this journey called life, is that even in Christ my life will not be easy, but it will be fruitful. I have the greatest living on the inside of me, so I can't give up. Once I stay connected to my power source which is the Word of God, prayer, worship and just talking to God, I am more than a conqueror. I am the child of the One who sits on the throne. There is nothing God cannot deliver me from. It may be His will for me to go through trials and tests, but I'm sure that it's working for my good. We all have learned something from our pain and struggles. God is not punishing us, but He's molding us to be better if you allow the potter to do His job.

I remember when I was giving birth to my daughter, I didn't have any medicine at all, so every time the contractions came, I felt every one of them. It was a pain I cannot describe, but I knew I had to endure the pain to deliver my daughter. After a few pushes, she finally came out and it was the greatest feeling to see your child who's been living inside of you for nine months. It's the same God you believed to cure our pain and replace it with joy. The pain was not there to defeat us or the make us feel as if God does not care, it's to develop us into something great. Even though it hurts, there is a good purpose in the pain. God has created us to be overcomers. That's why we must have endurance. Suffering through the pain has allowed us to grow and mature because it produces a better you in the end. Whatever you have had to endure throughout life, just know God does love you and He does have a plan that will bring forth much fruit and bring to you and expected end of joy and prosperity.

I am now a independent contractor and I have been doing hair transplants for 15 years. I have traveled the world and worked with many doctors and stayed in some of the best hotels. So yes, this same teenage mom who grew up living in the projects without her parents is traveling the world while getting paid, "look at God." All the stuff I have been through; the good, the bad, and the ugly, all worked together for my good. No matter what, God still had a plan for my life. Now I am a licensed minister at Greater Experience Church. I have been a co-author a few times and my book has made #1 on Amazon twice. God has blessed me to be an entrepreneur for 6 years. Look out for my newest venture called *TLheels Design Shoes*. God has truly blessed and saved my life.

If you would have told me I would be where I am today when I was a young child, I wouldn't have believed you. But that's the kind of God we serve. Another goal and dream that I have is to become a homeowner one day. Though life is not about material things, but there is nothing wrong with desiring good things. It is our heavenly Father's pleasure to bless His children with good things that bring glory to His name. My life has changed for the better and as long as I stay close to God, even when trouble comes He will allow you to overcome them and give you peace that surpasses all understanding.

According to *Merriam-Webster.com*, the definition for *endurance*, "is the ability to be able to withstand hardship or adversity." Adversity will come, but God's strength will be there to carry you through and cause you to triumph. Have you ever had to study for a test? I know some people are naturally smart and don't have to study, but there are people like you and me who has to stay up for hours studying in order to receive a passing grade.

Many highly paid positions such as doctors, lawyers, and nurses have difficult curriculums to pass. If it was so easy to be a doctor don't you think we would have an abundance of doctors? If it was so easy to become a nurse, there wouldn't be a lack of nurses. Not only do you have to be intelligent enough to pass the curriculum, but you have the will to endure a difficult course. You can't just say you want to be a surgeon overnight. That takes time, practice, patience and even some tears and many late nights of studying instead of partying and having a good time. God didn't intend for life to be so easy, but He did promise that we would reap what we sow. If you sow hard work and determination, you will reap the benefits of blessing and enjoy the fruit of your labor.

7
Love

This chapter is still being written in my life. I have accepted God's love for my life through Jesus Christ. The Bible declares in John 3:16 that "God so loved the world, that He gave His only begotten Son, that whosoever believes in Him, shall not perish but have everlasting life."

The first time I started reading the four Gospels of Jesus Christ, I cried. I cried because within those moments I felt God's love because I finally understood why Jesus died on the Cross and all He endured before He was crucified. It's during my study that I realized I've rejected His love towards me and for so long and I never even honored Him. I am emphasizing this point because it's what helps keep me as a single woman until the Lord blesses me to get married. I know my worth and my identity in Christ.

When I was in my early twenties, I didn't know what to look for in a man. I thought being in love was having sex and going from relationship to relationship. That was my normal because I didn't know my worth or who God created me to be. At one time, I never liked being alone. Now I enjoy being alone because God keeps me and gives me joy. I rather be alone than be in a stressful relationship. I've been waiting so many years for my husband since I got saved. I dated a few times, but it wasn't what God had for me. I'm very content being single because I know God's timing is perfect. I've learned to wait on God and trust Him in every area of life. I even commit my love life to Him, because He knows what is best for me.

Today, I am truly enjoying my life and the peace that God gives me because I've learned not to lean on my own understanding. Yes, waiting can be frustrating at times, but this one thing I know is true. I'd rather wait on the Lord than be in a hurry and make the wrong choice. I love God, and I know He loves me and wants the best for me. This is a source of encouragement for me knowing that my Father will bless me with a husband when He sees that this person is right to be with me. At the same time God is working on me inside and out to mold me into a Godly woman, prepared to be a good wife.

God wants the very best for His children. He doesn't want us to just settle for anyone or anything. That is why he said "do not be anxious for anything," but He wants us to pray about everything. God has a plan for our life. He is concerned about everything we do, even dating. In Proverbs 3:5-6, the Bible says for us to "…trust in the Lord with all our heart and to lean not to our own understanding, but in all our ways to acknowledge him, and He shall direct our paths." Well, I will admit, when I thought I was trusting in God, in fact, I was leaning to my own understanding. I know this because, the Bible teaches that God doesn't tempt anyone to do evil but we are drawn away by our own lustful desires. Many times we tell God when we're ready to date, instead of us asking Him, "Lord, are you ready for me to date."

Think about your past relationships, some we're very heartbreaking, some were lessons, and some were a waste of time. I remember I was dating, and I didn't hear God say anything. I didn't get a yes or no. However, it was after I left that relationship that God showed me, that whenever He is silent that means we should be still and wait on Him. Another thing the Lord revealed to me was, look at a person's characteristics. Do they line up on what I desired and prayed for? Do they line up with what the Bible says a godly person should be? I have so much peace knowing I'm waiting in my Father's perfect will. I'm no longer leaning to my own understanding with dating And being guided by my feelings. It's easy to get a cuddle buddy and a person to have fun with, but we must ask ourselves, are we really trusting God if we are being led by our emotions? One thing I know for sure is when God sends my husband to me, I will have peace about him. God would never send someone to me that would lead me away from the purpose and calling God has placed upon my life.

Now I know the meaning of love and my value in Christ, I'll keep waiting with joy For God to accomplish His perfect will in my life. Since God is love, we must understand what love is. The Bible declares,

> Love is patient, love is kind. It does not envy, it does not boast, it is not proud. It does not dishonor others, it is not self-seeking, it is not easily angered, it keeps no record of wrongs. Love does not delight in evil but rejoices with the truth. It always protects, always trusts, always hopes, always perseveres. Love never fails.
>
> 1 Cor. 13:4-8

I encourage those who are married, planning to get married or in a friendship, to keep no record of wrong doing. If you're going to decide to stay with someone, stop holding them captive by what they did in the past.

ABOUT THE AUTHOR

Evangelist Theresa Lawrence is a mom to Tamya Hibbler, she's God fearing, an entrepreneur for fashion and self-employed independent contractor for hair transplants where she works with various doctors across the world. Theresa Lawrence is known for her boldness for the Word of God and being a prayer warrior. She loves to talk, be friendly and treat others right. Although Theresa has had a challenging childhood, God has truly blessed her. That's why she knows what it's like to be an *Overcomer*. In this book you will see the challenges that Theresa has faced throughout her life with being a teen mom, in foster care and more. God has allowed her to overcome them all. I hope this book brings you encouragement, hope, and a sense of God's love. This book is about overcoming every obstacle and how God's love has redeemed me from my past.

ABOUT THE PUBLISHER

Let Life to Legacy bring your story to literary life! We offer the following publishing services: manuscript development, editing, transcription services, ghost-writing, cover design, copyright services, ISBN assignment, worldwide distribution, and eBook conversion.

Throughout production, we keep the author informed every step of the way. Even if you do not have a manuscript, that's not a problem for us. We can ghost-write your book from audio recordings or legible handwritten documents. Whether print-on-demand or trade publishing, we have packages to meet your publishing needs. At *Life to Legacy*, we take the stress out of becoming a published author.

Unlike other *so-called* publishers, we do more than just print books. Our books and eBooks are distributed to book buyers, distributors, and online retailers throughout the world—this is real publishing! Call us today for a free quote.

Please visit our website
www.Life2Legacy.com
or call us
708-272-4444

Send e-mail inquiries
Life2Legacybooks@att.net

www.ingramcontent.com/pod-product-compliance
Lightning Source LLC
Chambersburg PA
CBHW051712090426
42736CB00013B/2658